Dedication

I would like to dedicate this book to my husband Trevor and my son Nathan, who gave me the permission to share their intimate thoughts and feelings of loss and grief.

I also want to thank God for the love and strength which He has given me during this difficult time and continues to give to me through friends and family, but also directly through quiet moments.

Introduction

A number of readers have asked at book signing events, what the next book would be about and whether I would give a voice to the other members of the family, apart from the mum who had a significant voice in the first book, *Marley's Memoir: The Journey to an Irreversible Action and the Aftermath*. It was important to give focus to the mother as she played a key role on that fateful day whilst also giving an insight into the mind of Marley, how he got to the point where he took an action which impacted those who were close to him. In this book I would like to give some insight to the thoughts and feelings of Marley's dad Trevor and his brother Nathan, to complete the picture of how they felt at the time when this event took place. I felt that it was important to share the male perspective also of loss and grief. The majority of the book gives an insight on how the family of three navigated life after this traumatic event, which covers up to the first twelve months after losing Marley.

The reader will get some understanding of the character and personality of each member of the family and how the loss of Marley impacts them. The book also covers some of the challenges the family have had to face during this time and how they try to take steps forward. Watch out for my third and final book in the Loss and Grief series, "He Cares"

Living Without Marley

Majendi Jarrett

I hope you are inspired by this book from Majendi

Published by New Generation Publishing in 2023

Copyright © Majendi Jarrett 2023

First Edition

paperback ISBN: 9-781-80369-939-4
hardback ISBN: 9-781-80369-940-0
ebook ISBN: 9-781-80369-941-7

www.newgeneration-publishing.com

New Generation Publishing

Prologue

It was a cold, cloudy December morning when I experienced the most traumatic event of my life. I had woken up quite early as I usually do to have a quiet time of prayer, reading my Bible and a devotional. I read the verse of the day and then went on to read about a woman named Martha who was in a refugee camp and had experienced the traumatic loss of her family; rebels had broken into her home and killed her husband and two of her sons whilst she and her six-month-old son were hiding. I could not begin to imagine the pain and agony she must have gone through, and I was silently asking, "God, how could you have allowed this to happen?"

Little did I know that Martha's story was preparing me for what I would be facing in a little under two hours. I was also astounded by Martha's faith and joy which the author of the devotional wanted to bring to light. Despite the tragic loss of her family, she was full of joy supporting the other refugees in the camp and ministering to them.

I finished my quiet time and proceeded to get ready for work. It was a Friday, the end of my working week. I was looking forward to some downtime, but of course I had to get through Friday first.

As I prepared for working from home, I went downstairs to boot up my laptop, turn off the outside light and open the curtains. I was surprised that the light was still on, as this indicated that Marley had not left for his paper round. I checked the back door as is my usual routine but did not realise that the door was not locked until I came back downstairs the second time. I took out the washing from the washing machine with the intention of taking the bedsheets to hang outside when I came back downstairs.

The second time round, I noticed the back door leading to the garden was not locked with the key and I assumed that my younger son had left it unlocked after leaving for his paper round early in the morning. I thought he had got up when I went back upstairs.

I went back upstairs again and finished off getting ready whilst informing my husband that the back door was unlocked and our youngest must have left it open in his rush not to be late for his paper round.

I was back downstairs for the third time and, since it was cloudy and cold, I thought I would only hang out the bedsheet and put the rest of the clothing on the clothes airer.

I grabbed the navy-blue bed sheet, opened the door leading to the garden from the utility room and saw something that no mother ever wants to see. *Was I awake?* I asked myself. *Am I really seeing what I am seeing? Is it my imagination or is the sight in front of me real? I must be in a trance as this cannot be real. It is not true; it must be a mirage.* In those few seconds, which felt like hours, I refused to accept that what I was seeing was reality. I felt I must still be asleep and having a nightmare.

I was in shock, I could not move for those few seconds and then I shouted, "Marley, Marley!" and the sound of my voice did not even seem like mine. I ran towards the mirage, which unfortunately was reality.

Contents

Chapter One

Navigating a New Normal – Mum's View

It does not matter how many sessions you have with a therapist, or books you read or what friends and family who may have gone through similar events say, your situation will always be unique to you. The way in which you navigate it will be unique to you. The pain you will feel on a daily basis will be unique to you. No one can prepare you for the mood swings or the low mood because the relationship you share with that loved one is unique to you. Don't get me wrong, you will definitely take some pointers from all what you read or sessions you attend but you will need to make it your own. By this I mean, finding what works for you. What works for you and those around you who shared in the pain and loss will be unique to each of you.

Every day will be tough, trying to make sense of it all, continuously questioning yourself. Drifting between reality and the surreal, not sure if you are sleeping, thinking that you are having a nightmare that you would wake up and realise it was not real. No relief from waking up and realising it was just a bad dream because unfortunately it is real, it did happen, this person is no longer here, and you have to live life without them. The thought of not holding, touching, speaking with them will almost break you in two. You will question life, *what is it all about?* Rushing around doing things that in the face of loss becomes insignificant, you will question your ambitions and the things you had held as important or invaluable, are they worth it? These are some of the questions which will be going round and round in your head.

The time you spend on certain things will become irrelevant and you will try to reprioritise all over again. You will question the pressure you put on others to do things in a certain way, live a certain way and achieve ambitions all over again. *Is it worth it?* This will be the question you will ask yourself over and over again? *Why?* Because we do not take any of the accolades or material things we chase and work hard for when we leave this world. I remember some years back reading a book by Clayton M. Christensen, *"How will you measure your life?"* My manager at the time had given each of us in the team this book to guide us as we formed a new team. After reading the book it emerged that the most important thing in our lives is the relationship we have with others. The way someone felt after an encounter with us. It is not what you achieve academically or professionally that counts with those who are close to you but how you made them feel. I think a lot about how Marley felt. Had he thought that he had my time and attention?

When I walk by the shops in our local area – where our local Co-op grocery store is located – I would see the newsagents, and after a few more steps I would be by the local pizza shop, the charity shop, and finally, I would be by the chicken and chip shop. What do all these shops have in common? At one time or the other, in the previous year, Marley had been there. The newsagent would definitely get the highest score because he was there every day for his paper round. I cannot help but think that these are the same sidewalks where Marley walked just twelve months ago. Do I get emotional as these thoughts flood my mind? Of course I do. Does it make me want to run away and not experience it? No way! If anything, it takes me closer to him.

I imagine him going to the Co-op grocery store to get some crisps or a drink. I imagine the many times he went into the newsagent, not only to do his paper round but to get something. There were times when he got me a birthday card or Mother's Day card from there. Other times he got his snacks and energy drinks from there. I recall a few times when he had said, "It seems I am spending all the money I earn from the paper round in the newsagent. I need to go somewhere else." He would go somewhere else but then he would be back again spending his few pounds in the same shop where he earned it. It was very convenient. I felt the same. I have memories of Marley in this local, in this town, and although it can be emotional sometimes, I can't imagine myself being anywhere else. Definitely not. I would go to the shopping centre in our small town. I would go to the same bank, the very same one I introduced to Marley. I would go to the same supermarket and sometimes take the same route which he rode his bike after school or after the few times he had visited the game shop. It's almost as if I could see him peddling on his bike, going as fast as he could so he could get to the sanctuary of his room. There are times when I passed him on the road and even though I would toot him, he would not hear because he had his headphones on, or he was so focused on getting home that he would not hear anything else in his surroundings.

Chapter Two

Losing my Son – Dad's View

My name is Trevor and I am Marley's dad. I would describe myself as a simple person. I usually say, "I don't want no fuss, no complication. I like to be in the background and not be in the spotlight." I would say that I have been like this since I was a child. I try to keep on the straight and narrow to avoid "rocking the boat", as rocking the boat means that I would be in the spotlight and I don't want to be in the spotlight, not before this event and certainly not now.

When the events of 11 December 2020 took place, it threw me completely out of my comfort zone. (If you don't know the event I am referring to, you need to read *Marley's Memoir: The Journey to an Irreversible Action and the Aftermath.*) The invasion of outsiders (by outsiders meaning the police, forensics and paramedics into our home), the questions, and the constant footfalls in and out for over two hours was unbearable. I remembered lying in bed the morning of 11 December 2020. I saw my wife going through her usual routine of getting ready for work, then she went downstairs and then back upstairs. I recalled drifting in and out of sleep. I had fallen asleep when my nap was interrupted with her on and off conversations. I vaguely heard her say something about Marley leaving the outside light on when he left for his paper round, but it all seemed far away.

Suddenly, I was abruptly brought back to full awareness by her cry: "Trevor, quickly come downstairs, it's Marley." My immediate thought was that Marley had been hit by a car as he rode out of the drive from home to go on his paper round. I remembered thinking how many times I had told him that he came out of the drive too fast without knowing who might be coming down the footpath. With a thumping heart and unsteady hands, I got out of bed as I could hear a cry from my wife, which I had never heard before. Something was seriously wrong as she kept insisting that I should hurry downstairs.

I succeeded in putting on jogging bottoms and a hoodie and went downstairs. I was not expecting to see Marley in that position. I knew immediately that he was no longer with us. I did not want to go there. At the insistence of my wife, I had no choice but to go there. In my mind, a man is expected to be brave, fearless, be the leader, take charge and be a protector. I had to do this, *I could do this*, is what I kept saying to myself. Later I recalled standing there in the garden looking at this sight that I did not want to see, and, in my heart, I wanted to run and hide. Unfortunately, I couldn't, I had to man up. So with a masque of bravery to disguise my turbulent feelings I moved towards the vision on the tree. I had no choice but to do what my wife was asking: "Please get him off the tree," she said. I tried but I could not, so I asked her for scissors and then everything became surreal. There I was with my youngest son in my hands, cold as ice. I could not bear to hold him any longer so I put him down on the lawn, but I soon heard my wife saying, "Don't leave him on the grass, bring him inside." I tried telling her that he was gone but she was not listening to me, she was on the phone to the emergency services asking for an ambulance.

Together with his brother Nathan, we brought him in and laid him on the utility floor. It was devastating to see my wife lying over Marley, praying fervently for him to get up, for the life that she already knew was gone from him to fill him up. I believe in God but in my mind, I felt that this was an impossible task, even for God; or was it that my faith was not as strong as my wife's? Whilst I was contemplating this, the paramedics arrived and moved us out of the area. All I could think about was that this could not be happening. It had felt like only a few minutes ago when I was drifting in and out of sleep, enjoying the bed all to myself to be abruptly pushed into the reality of this situation. Thoughts such as *Why would Marley do this?* kept going through my mind. When the paramedic confirmed that Marley was gone, I was numbed. I could not cry or scream. I would have liked to break something even though I was not one to express emotions in that way. I looked at my wife and Nathan and they were in pieces. Totally heartbroken and I envied the way they could just express their feelings freely. I had to be strong for them. I was the man of the home, the protector of his family even though I was very far from feeling like a protector at the moment. I was feeling like a failure. *How could I not have seen this coming? How did I miss this?* Only the night before I was speaking to him about what he needed to do when he went to the bank. Marley had even posted a video clip of the press-ups his mum had encouraged him to do daily. *Where were the signs that night that I missed?* These were some of the questions going through my mind.

My wife was falling apart, and, in a way, I envied her that she could just let it all out whilst I felt as if I was being suffocated and could not breathe, but I kept telling myself I had to be strong. I remembered putting my arms around her, consoling her. I felt helpless but at least I could give her a hug. We sat down by the dining table just looking at each other, trying to make sense of this nightmare. During this time the police had arrived and wanted to check his room, they wanted details on what happened and statements for their records. It felt like a very long day, but it all went very quickly. As much as I wanted it to be a bad dream, unfortunately it was reality.

I kept being hit by this strong sense of guilt, feeling that I could have been a better father to Marley. I had not been very accommodating with Marley's ups and downs, especially in the weeks and months leading to his demise. I know I am not a very patient person. I am also very traditional in the way I see life in that children should respect elders, especially their parents. When I was growing up it was the norm to greet your parents in the morning and others around you. It was a sign of respect. These were the principles Marley and I did not agree on. Marley rebelled against these traditions, and we were always at loggerheads. It meant that our father and son relationship was not smooth running – more so in the preceding year, it was almost non-existent because I was not very accommodating of bad behavior. Maybe it had something to do with the relationship I had with my father, but that's another story for another day.

I was constantly telling Marley off because he was not being respectful. When he wanted my help with something or the other, I was reluctant to give it to him. I remembered the evening before when Marley had asked me for a haircut, and I had ignored him. In my mind, he always chose the wrong time to ask for help. I would be available all day but the requests for a haircut were only made when I wanted to watch football, relax, or to watch something on TV. I was from the generation where children worked round the schedules of their parents and not the other way round. In my generation there was no way growing up, I would have expected my dad to work to my schedule. When I thought about having refused to cut his hair, it fills me with regret knowing that Marley was no longer here. I was gutted. I remembered lying in bed that night and saying to my wife, "Why do you think he wanted to have a haircut on Thursday night?"

"No idea," she had said.

This is one of many questions that still haunts me twelve months after the event. Honestly, I wished I could just have a good cry but unfortunately the tears were all internal, mingled with pain and guilt. I started questioning myself as I have done several times: *Was I a good father?* I didn't think I was. I was not the touchy, feely type like my wife. I remembered giving the boys handshakes when they were kids as a joke. My intention was to make them tough; in my mind they needed to be strong. Touchy and emotional stuff made you weak was my thinking at the time. It was okay for women to be touchy feely, I had thought. Of course, my views have since changed, but I had held on to those views for a long time and that must have shaped my relationship with Marley. When I think back, Marley just wanted someone to listen to him and give some constructive feedback, but my immediate response was always to tell him to be tough. Other times I would listen but without actually hearing him, which eventually led to Marley's withdrawal and instead sought out his mother for emotional support. Besides that, I am not a natural conversationalist, I am a man of few words and trying to give words of support was well out of my comfort zone. On the other hand, if there were practical problems such as fixing a toy, or a punctured tyre on a bike, I would be the man you could call on.

The emotional stuff I left for my wife. She had a lot more comforting words to say than I did. It was this – among other reasons – that I found it hard to make the phone call to my family to tell them what had happened. *What could I say?* How could I start such a difficult conversation as I did not know what to say at the time. How could I tell my mum, Marley's Nan, who was almost ninety at the time, that her grandson had done this? How could I tell my sisters of this devastation? How do you even put the words together? This was taken out of my control when a friend who was driving passed the house saw all the police cars outside and called to ask me what was up? Without thinking about it I told him what had happened, and it was only afterwards I realised what I had done.

The devastating news was now out of the confines of our home and could travel like wildfire from one house to the other, from one person to the other. I was obviously not thinking clearly or it was the relief to speak to another adult male, I honestly don't know why I told him. The narrative was now out of our control and we needed to inform family and friends before they found out through the grapevine as these things had a way of travelling from one person to another. My wife was not happy and told me I had to immediately call my sister who lived close to our mum so that she could go over and break the news before one of their friends said something. I was reluctant to make the call as I did not know how she would take it. In the end my wife made the call and put it in such a way that whilst it was a shock, it was handled with the care that I knew she was capable of, and I was not. My sister was given the task of telling the rest of the family on my side as my wife had to break the news to her side of the family.

That night lying in bed I could not get to sleep. Neither could my wife because our minds and thoughts were so full of the event from the morning. It spanned the whole day, and it did not matter how much we wanted to block it out, it was like an unwanted guest which was not taking the hint to leave. In the end we gave up trying to sleep and talked. We had been told not to think about what we could have done better or how things could have been different as this sort of thinking would make us feel worse and there was nothing, we could do about it. It also stopped us from starting a blame game. I had looked at her lying there beside me, and I wondered what she was thinking. Did she think it was my fault? I would not blame her, knowing that I could have done more. I could have been more understanding of what Marley was going through as I felt that in some ways Marley was very similar to me in personality and character.

I had found school in England very challenging as a teenager. I had arrived in England at the age of fourteen from Barbados and was thrown into a very different society and culture from what I was used to. In those days there were not many black,

West Indian children with strong Caribbean accents in my school, so it was a culture shock to me and my peers who treated me to some extent as if I was an alien. Fortunately for me, unlike Marley, I was really good at sport, and cricket was my passion, so I could distract myself from playing cricket and also connect with other like-minded people. These are some of the thoughts that went through my mind as we went through the preparation for the funeral and also in the days and weeks leading to the inquest. I had tried several times to share my experience with Marley when he had complained about school and not having friends. Unfortunately, on each occasion I had tried to share my experience, my words had not had the desired impact. I was more of a fixer than a talker so whatever I tried to say did not come out right and it ended with Marley saying, "It's not the same, my situation is different from yours. You cannot compare your experience with what I am going through." I thought it was best if I kept quiet and left my wife to deal with it as I knew she was better at this than I was.

I don't know how I went through the viewing and the funeral as I was reluctant to go anywhere near the funeral home, even for the meetings to discuss the arrangements. It was very hard for me, and I may be called a coward, but I just could not go there. Fortunately, the pastor went with my wife and Nathan and my sister came over to be with me whilst they were gone. I was going through the motions of getting up, fixing whatever needed to be fixed as directed by my wife and then distracting myself with football. There was a lot of distraction from football as the team I supported, Manchester United, was underperforming. I would tune into all the forums on YouTube and watch the rematch on TV and this was a good distraction for me as the day of the funeral approached. I remembered going to the viewing with the family, but it all felt unreal. I felt like a robot. I was just going through the motions, but it was not sinking in.

On the day of the funeral, it really hit me. I could not

hold it back; the tears came out like a flood. I was supposed to be strong for my wife and son but as soon as we got to the church the thought of Marley lying in the coffin broke something within me. I was glad I had dark glasses to hide my tears. I could not stop the tears flowing down my cheeks even if I tried. The reality of Marley's passing really hit me. I cried all throughout the service until we got to the cemetery. Afterwards I tried to forget by watching football.

In the days that followed, I tried to discourage my wife, Jenny from watching and listening to videos of Marley on her phone, but she was not having it. She said that watching the videos help her cope with her loss. It was the opposite for me as it made me really sad. I could not listen to or watch videos in those early days. There was still the inquest to come. If it was left to me, I would not have attended the opening of the inquest even though it was by a video link. After the opening of the inquest, I thought that was it. No, there was the inquest itself when we got to hear all the details read over again. It was torture going through the hearing. I really did not want to be part of it. At this time, I had been having counselling as my wife had insisted – we all needed to do it. I had wanted it to be group therapy, but we were told it was best to do individual therapy and if later we needed group therapy, we could ask for it. It was not easy talking to someone about how I felt; it's not what I do. I forced myself to stick with it and succeeded in doing the eight sessions. Looking back, I think it actually helped me to be more open about how I was feeling and not to internalise everything. It helped that afterwards I could talk about it with my wife and Nathan.

The inquest was tough as this was held about three months after the event. It was about the time when I had started to adjust a bit to the new normal. Suddenly, I was plunged back into that day on 11 December and the devastating event was being recited minute by minute, hour by hour. It was very difficult for all of us. It was a very difficult hour. I tried to tune myself out and only paid attention when my wife needed to make a response, which was not very often. I honestly did not see the point of the inquest as we all knew what had happened; *would it change anything?* No, nothing would change; it would not bring Marley back. I was glad when it was over, and we could put it behind us. I was able to breathe easily when we got off the video call. We had hugged each other in a family group hug as we tried to put what we had heard behind us.

The following months I tried to get through some form of normalcy, but it was not easy. Everywhere I turned, I was reminded of that day. Being in the utility room where I had laid Marley when I brought him in from the garden kept giving me flashbacks. At the beginning of the year, we had a leak in the family bathroom, and it made a mess of the kitchen ceiling. We decided it would be a good time to do a bit of decorating as Marley's fingerprints were all over the walls in the hallway and the kitchen because it was his habit of always putting his fingers on the walls after tinkering with his bike. Almost every wall in our home had some imprint from Marley. We got some paint, and it was my task to put fresh paint on the walls. In a way it gave me something to focus on, something to keep me busy and distract me from my thoughts. I could do something practical.

Chapter Three

Losing my Brother – Brother's View

My name is Nathan and I am the older brother to Marley Asher Adeshino Prescott. Up until the 10 December 2020, I would say that I had had a good life. And although I had lost people who were close to me, like my granddad, nothing could have prepared me for the loss of my brother. I was not prepared. We had spent so much time together growing up, and although I knew as we entered adulthood things would change, I still felt that no matter how different we were we would always be there for each other. It was only a few months leading up to December that we were talking about when we would get married, and how our children would hang out and play together like we did as kids. Little did I know at the time that this was never going to happen. I did not realise how much I loved my brother until he was no longer there to do all the things that at the time, I had taken for granted.

I remembered waking up that morning to the cries of our mum from somewhere outside my bedroom door. "Trevor, Nathan, please come and get Marley off the tree!" I had heard her cry and so I quickly put on my jogging bottoms and ran downstairs forgetting to put on a tee shirt until I got outside and felt the cold air. As soon as I got outside, I knew something was very wrong. My whole world seemed to cave in at that moment. I could not even go near him; instead, I started pacing the length of the garden, going round and round in circles, no longer aware of the cold morning air. As tears ran down my cheeks, my hands on my head full of despair, all I was able to say was, "Why? Why? Why?" *How could I have missed it?* I was downstairs with him late the night before and there was nothing to indicate that he would do this. He had been sitting at the dining table eating his pizza just before I came downstairs to put the dishwasher on. For some reason we had not spoken to each other that evening, as Marley was watching something on his laptop. Without so much as a word, Marley had taken the last piece of pizza he was eating from the plate and handed it to me, to put in the dishwasher.

Later when I was in bed, I had heard him go back downstairs but did not think anything of it. Thinking back, I wondered if that was the time when these negative thoughts had gotten hold of him. If only I had gone downstairs when I heard him, *would I have been a welcome distraction?* I wondered. I kept beating myself up about it wondering *if only?* This guilt or blame would continue long after the funeral. It was at the inquest when I learned for the first time that he had said something about having suicide ideation when drinking alcohol. I kept thinking what I could have done after he had told me that he had bought alcohol on his eighteenth birthday? *Was that when he had bought the alcohol, he had drank a week later?* Was there anything I could have done to stop him? At the time I had not thought much of it as I thought buying alcohol at the age of eighteen confirmed your adult status. If only I could have seen into the future. I had my parents but I felt alone; I had lost my sibling – my confidante. We talked and shared so much, yet Marley had never let on that he was having suicidal thoughts.

When I saw something on social media which I thought was funny I would share it with Marley. If I watched something on Netflix, I would tell him about it. When an artist released a single or an album I liked, I would tell him about it as we shared similar tastes. Though there was almost a four-year age gap between us, Marley understood the vibes of our generation. I lost all of this when he was no longer there. Now, I had to depend on my friends or my parents, which was not the same as when Marley was there. Marley had always been in my room, moaning about something or the other. It was not easy at times as I wanted my privacy and sometimes when he got silly, I would ask him to leave my room. How I longed for those days when he would be in my room talking nonsense about this or that. Unfortunately, those days would never come back, they were gone.

It saddens me that I did not value those days at the time and now I would never have them again. It has been very difficult going through the grieving period as it appears that everywhere I turned a young person had lost their lives, either ending it themselves or they had been the victim of a shooting or stabbing. I don't seem to be able to hide from it. It's on the news when my mum turns on the TV, it's on social media, it's everywhere. It seems that everyone has been touched by someone with some form of mental illness.

I was quite moved by the young man who was only nineteen years old and was found dead in a pond in a forest in London. It was a flashback to that rawness and freshness of loss; it brought back how I felt in those early days and reminded me that although it felt as if I was still in the same space I was actually moving forward, though very slowly. I did not want to think about the Christmas after Marley passed or the preparation for the funeral. The funeral itself was too hard. I sometimes feel embarrassed when I think of how I lost it at the graveside. The reality of it all hit me whilst I was standing by the grave, seeing the coffin descending, knowing that my baby brother who I had known for all his eighteen years was no longer with us. I could not control my legs. All of a sudden, my legs became wobbly, and I could barely keep myself upright. I was sobbing uncontrollably, and I did not care who was looking at me or heard me. I was glad my mum led me away from it all so that I could no longer see the coffin in the grave.

No one can prepare you for the loss of someone close to you. When the hearse had arrived at our house it was my mum who was falling apart. I was the one who consoled her all the way to the church for the service, and now the table had turned around. She was the one who consoled me. Afterwards, it was a relief to get home and just be with my parents. Knowing that we had gone through the hardest part was like a weight off my shoulders, although nothing could be compared to that Friday morning. Neither the funeral nor the inquest could compare to that terrible Friday morning when our world was turned upside down. That Friday would forever be imprinted in my mind, and the smell of that day would sometimes come vividly to me. Helping my dad carry Marley inside – his wet clothes, which were soaked from a bit of rain and probably his body fluids – will stay with me forever.

My first birthday without Marley was much better than I had thought. Mum decided that we should have McDonald's since it was a Saturday, and we should watch video recordings of happier times with Marley when we had gone on holiday to Barbados and Florida. She wanted to transfer some of these recordings from a camcorder to her phone, so she would have easy access to it. I was the person delegated with this task. My dad and I had thought at first that it would be difficult to watch the videos of Marley. My first thoughts were this is not how I wanted to spend my birthday. It turned out to be very comforting as we went back to the days when we were very young, on our first family holiday in Barbados, my dad's place of birth. I remembered that holiday as if it was yesterday, staying up later than our usual bedtime, meeting family for the first time and having lots of fizzy drinks and junk food at our disposal. Also being able to see the younger Nathan and how forward I was compared to now, I thought I was a bit more reserved now than I was in my early years. In the end I was able to transfer quite a few memories from the camcorder to mum's phone and in the process refreshed my memory of the good times I had with Marley.

When I reflect on those early days after the funeral, one of the things I would recommend to anyone who has suffered the tragic loss of a loved one is counselling. Just to talk to someone else, especially someone you don't know, can be comforting. At first, I was very reluctant to talk to a stranger about personal stuff. After some persuasion from mum, I gave in. My intention was to try one session and if I felt uncomfortable, I would withdraw from further counselling. My first session was good, and I was given some coping mechanism which helped me to deal with the pain and loss. I attended all eight sessions and also put in for a further two as the therapist advised me, I would need more sessions after the inquest. The therapist also helped me to think about how I would like to remember Marley. I had several ideas and one of which I would take forward in the coming months.

It was around that time when mum first told me about the foundation she wanted to start as a legacy to Marley and return to the book that she had started writing in 2019. I thought it was great that she had these two ideas to focus on as she had been really down. Whilst she had the desire to look deeper into Marley's phone to get some answers and research for the book, I had no desire to dig deeper into Marley's past. My dad and I had decided not to look deeper into what Marley was thinking at the time and why he did what he did. Maybe in a way I might be called a coward, but I did not want to come across something that would be upsetting for me. Mum had shared with me some of her discoveries after accessing Marley's phone. She said it gave her some understanding of Marley's state of mind. I had also kept quite a few of the WhatsApp voice messages which Marley had sent to me over time. I had forwarded the messages to her since she said it would also give her some clarity. Unfortunately, around this time, I kept getting a type of vertigo which kept me in bed for two to three days at a time. It was very worrying for me and my parents as we did not understand what the root cause was. I would be fine one minute and the next minute I was unsteady on my feet due to bouts of dizziness which made me feel nauseous. I had four episodes in the space of ten months before we identified a root cause. It was difficult for all of us at this time, especially since we were still recovering from the unexpectedness of Marley's passing and we did not have the strength to deal with another unknown.

Chapter Four

Let's Have Therapy – Mum's View

One thing I would recommend after a tragedy or traumatic event is counselling. It can be very daunting talking to a stranger about deep and personal things which you might not even be able to discuss with someone who you are close to. I was not very keen on the idea when it was suggested to me by friends and family and others who had walked the road I was on. I decided to give it a try and also encouraged my family to do the same. There was reluctance from Trevor and Nathan, which was not surprising. If I was finding it hard to make that first step, I knew that Trevor and Nathan would find this even more difficult. I knew if we were going to do this then it would be down to me to make the calls and link up the respective therapist to each of us.

I focused on Trevor as he was the one who seemed to have kept all his emotions inside and I knew that although he was not saying it, he was hurting. Every night before going to sleep, if you could call snippets of shut eye here and there sleep, he would open up a bit. I was able to get some idea of the unfounded guilt and blame he had harboured. He had said a few times that "he was not a good father and that he could have done more for Marley". I would stop him immediately from going down that guilt ridden trap. "There are things that you are good at and there are things that I am good at," I would say. We were together in this. As parents we were not in competition; if I did something for Marley it was for both of us, and if he did something for Marley, then it was for both of us. Whilst I had been good at the emotional and touchy-feely stuff, he had been quite good at the physical, action driven stuff.

Trevor was the first one to start therapy sessions. I had paired him with someone who I hoped would push him a bit out of his comfort zone and get him to open up. After his first session, he said it was helpful. I could hear him laughing when I walked past the bedroom; I thought if he had the right person, he would find it beneficial. I was not sure if he would attend all eight sessions, but I was happy that he had started and seemed to be getting something from it. After three sessions he was given some exercise to channel his grief, which he had to do in between sessions. At first, he was not sure what the benefit was, but I encouraged him to do it and gradually he started to get something out of it.

With Nathan it took a bit more effort to get him to agree to see a therapist as he did not see what the point of it was. He kept saying he was fine and did not think that the sessions would add any value. After trying different tactics, he was still unwilling to engage, so I used my trump card. I told him that refusing therapy reminded me of Marley not wanting to engage in counselling. I was not below using any tactics I could to get him at least to try it. It was in the same way he did not want to get help because he thought he did not need it. This actually did the trick. We agreed that he would at least do one session and if he did not want to do any more, I would not force him. Again, I was very fortunate that the therapist I had paired him with, was someone who could relate to him. His sessions were Saturday mornings, which worked well for him and after the first session he agreed to have another one. It was also helpful that it was a phone call and not a video call, like Trevor and I had engaged in. Nathan could talk to her almost as if he was speaking to someone he knew because he could not see her.

When I had my first session with my therapist, I realised that she was best suited to me. She would ask a question and then allow me the time to respond, which would result in me giving her far more than I realised. She would make notes and then asked me a further question about what I had said. In this way she allowed me to open up. Around this time, I was finding it very hard to sleep for longer than three hours without waking up. If I went to bed around midnight, I would still wake up between 1.30 and 2 o'clock in the morning, and I would find it really hard to go back to sleep as I would be thinking of Marley. My thoughts would take me back to the timeline of what he was doing around that time on that fateful morning. I would eventually go back to sleep, but I would wake up again around 3am and would stay awake until 4 or sometimes 5 o'clock in the morning.

The first few nights after the event, a friend recommended herbal sleeping pills. I took the minimum dose, but it did nothing, I still woke up at the same time. I took the maximum dosage, and it did nothing, I still woke up at the same time. I stopped taking the pills and around this time the nurse from the doctor's surgery reached out and asked if there was anything we needed. I said I could not sleep and had not had a good sleep since the event. I was prescribed a different herbal sleeping pill which also was non-effective. When I shared my sleeping pattern with my therapist, she gave me an insight into why I was waking up around this time. According to her theory, I was trying to save Marley from what he did. This was based on the fact that when I woke up, I would think about all the actions and steps he took; it was as if I could see and hear him walking down the stairs, opening the door leading to the garden, taking the chairs to the bottom of the tree, and then testing for height. These thoughts kept going round and round in my head and when I shared this with my therapist, she said it was the motherly desire to protect and save Marley. I had this strong desire in my subconscious to stop him from going through with his action and this was what would cause me to wake up around the time he had taken those steps, because in my subconscious, I still thought I could prevent what had happened.

In one of my sessions, I also shared that if someone should knock on the door who resembled Marley and told me that he was the real Marley I would believe it. She told me that it was that protective nature of not wanting to believe and accept that Marley could have taken this irreversible action.

Whilst my therapist really encouraged me to talk about the traumatic event, Trevor's therapist focused a lot on his relationship with his parents and siblings. She wanted him to discuss his upbringing – the first fourteen years of his life in Barbados and then his relationship with his children and his wife. It is quite interesting that she focused on these aspects as it was what he needed but did not realise it. He was constantly self-reflecting on his relationship with Marley, and what he could have done better, and so it was essential for him to reflect on the affinity he had with his dad and whether that had any bearing on his relationship with his sons.

After our sessions, sometimes, we would share some parts of our therapy sessions and he would say, "I wonder why she asks me about what happened?"

"Does your therapist ask you about your upbringing and relationships?" I would respond.

"No, my therapist was more focused on what happened and how that has affected my sleep."

He thought he was not getting anything out of it because the discussion was more focused on his early life, growing up and going to school. I would tell him that the therapist was probably trying to find similarities to his relationships and school life with Marley's. From his viewpoint he did not think he got much out of it, but I thought differently as it helped us as a family to talk more openly.

I recall one occasion telling my therapist that the things I thought would make me emotional had no effect, whilst the normal or ordinary things were what usually set me off. She gave me a really good insight into this; the normal or ordinary things are no longer normal or ordinary because Marley is no longer part of it. Things such as preparing my porridge for breakfast or putting croissants in the oven would set me off because Marley was usually part of that routine. We would both be competing for the microwave or the oven and most of the time he would beat me to it so that I had to wait for him before I did my bit. Without him, it was like a new normal and I was finding it hard to navigate this new normal as he was no longer a part of it. This was setting me off. Familiar songs from church would also set me off as I would get flashbacks of taking Marley and Nathan to church and singing these songs. On the other hand, going to the cemetery and putting flowers on the grave, liaising with the funeral masons for the headstone did not act as a trigger. It was confusing for me. I had sixteen sessions in total and whilst it was beneficial, I was glad when it ended. Whilst talking about the traumatic event was helpful, it was also very draining to me emotionally. I would finish therapy and have a really good cry. Maybe that was a good thing as it gave me the outlet to let it all out.

I was still struggling with my sleep. After the insight from the therapist, I succeeded in sleeping through until 3 o'clock in the morning. Around this time, I had access to the Campaign Against Living Miserably (CALM), one of the sources of support my employer had made available to me. I had three sessions with the sleep coach which helped. Some of the suggestions were breathing exercises which a friend of mine had also shared with me. When I woke up, I would pray, do the breathing exercises and it would calm my thoughts and help me get back to sleep. Another was listening to the different sounds or stories being read but these were sometimes too short, and it would finish before I had gone back to sleep. I decided to try going to sleep with the radio on as I discovered that when I slept with a background noise and woke up during the night, I could easily go back to sleep as I would not start thinking about the event of December 2020. Waking up to silence caused me to immediately start thinking of what had happened and then I found it hard to go back to sleep. My sleeping pattern improved after trying this.

Trevor was finding it hard to sleep through the night as well. His sleep was not as erratic as there were times when I would wake up and I would lie for hours listening to him breathing in and out. His problem was that when he woke up, he did not feel rested. He was sometimes more tired than before he had slept. He would go to sleep with his earphones on, listening to some comedy on YouTube and when he woke up, he would still be tired.

Nathan's sleeping pattern was messed up also but in a different way. He usually went to bed late but because of everything that had happened, he found it hard to fall asleep until the early hours of the morning. When he was not working it was alright but when he started working it was a challenge to get up for work. Fortunately, he had a late start, so he did not have to get up early in the morning.

Chapter Five

Marley's Legacy: Turning Lemon to Lemonade – Mum's View

As a mother or even as parents we have ambitions for our children. What they will achieve, what careers they will have, what they will do in life, who they will marry and how they will raise their children. It is very difficult to lose someone who was physically sick, more so someone who was physically healthy and had no known illness. When tragedy strikes, you feel that you are left with nothing; all the dreams and hopes you had for that person are gone with them and it feels that you are left with nothing except this pain and loss. This sense of pain and loss can be felt in different ways; you may become depressed and stay in that period of grief; you could be in denial and stay in that state of unbelief or you could try to channel the ambition you had for that person in a positive action. I have gained more understanding why people who had suffered a great loss become motivated to channel their efforts into a good cause.

I can totally relate to why they do it. I totally get it now. I remember a few hours after we had shared with close family the traumatic loss of Marley and someone close to me said, "When life gives you lemons, you make lemonade." At the time I had no idea what that meant. I knew it was about taking something bad and turning it into something good, but I was steeped in grief and could not see beyond that. How could I? My baby was no longer with us. A few days later someone else said something similar to me. Exactly a week later I woke up in the morning and I had this strong impression that I would start something in Marley's name as a legacy to him. It was very clear in my mind that it would be connected to art or animation or both, which he loved, and it would also be connected to anxiety and social disorder, which he suffered from. I wrote my thoughts down and decided I would look into this later, after the burial.

A month or so after the funeral I spoke to someone from a local charity who was giving me support to navigate the aftermath of this traumatic event. We had calls once every two weeks. She had asked me how I would like to remember Marley and I had shared with her what my thoughts were. She encouraged me to speak to the CEO of an organisation which supported young people who had similar issues to what Marley had. Around the same time, I had started a conversation with the principal of Marley's former secondary school. It was becoming much clearer how I could turn this "lemon into lemonade". I did not want to do just a one-off activity. It had to have longevity, so I had to think and plan carefully. Although making a one-off activity such as a bench in the park or donating to a charity that cares for young people with anxiety would have been good, in my opinion it was not enough. It was not what I was looking for. After speaking to the CEO of the organisation it became clear that they would play an important part in whatever I did for Marley's legacy.

I shared my thoughts with Trevor and Nathan as they needed to be involved, but in what capacity was not very clear at the time. I had a few more calls with the CEO who linked me up with other people in her organisation who had set up charities in the past. As I was not qualified in psychological therapies, I knew that I would need to involve people who were qualified to work directly with the target beneficiaries.

I could create a platform to raise the provision and provide aid for this. Marley's Child Trust Fund had been given to me as the next of kin and whilst I could have just given it to any organisation associated with young people, I held on to it as it made sense that it should be part of the startup funds for his legacy. I had never set up a charity before or been a trustee for a charity, so I had a lot of reading to do and research to ensure that I was doing the right thing.

I remember in those early days reaching out to sources which I thought would give some directions. Sources such as my local bank had no idea what was involved in opening an account for a charitable organisation. I knew I needed an account for the charity, but they could not advise on setting up the charity. They pointed me to the Citizens Advice Bureau (CAB), who pointed me to the Charity Commission website. Of course, I knew the website was there with a lot of information which at first reading did not make sense, hence the reason why I was reaching out to someone who I could speak to. I thought that was my first realization that this was not going to be easy. I pushed through because anything worth doing is never easy. There were lots of information on the charity commission website, and I started breaking it down into parts to make sense of it. One of the contacts from the CEO helped me to understand the different types of charities and how they could be set up. This was just a one-hour call, but it gave me so much insight on what I wanted and what I did not want.

I was now clear on what I wanted, and I had to identify who would be involved. It was a given that Nathan, Marley's brother, would be part of this. We brainstormed on who the other likely trustees would be. There were one or two people who had already registered an interest to be involved if I decided to do something. There were others who I believed should be part of it because they had been part of Marley's life from the very beginning: his godmother Jennifer, and his cousin Emma. I reached out to the potential trustees outlining what the charity would be set up for and to let me know if they wanted to be part of it. It was not enough that I wanted them to be part of it, they needed to want it also.

On acceptance we had a meeting in which I set out what the charity would do and how we would achieve this. I also shared what funds we had to start off with but of course we needed to generate more if we were to succeed in our objectives. I knew even before we brainstormed that there would be a charity fund-raising walk in Marley's name around the time of his birthday, but exactly what that would look like still needed to be defined. We brainstormed on other ideas and one of the trustees put forward the idea that she wanted to lose 7kg during the seventh month of Marley's passing. She had an objective to raise seven hundred pounds, and, in the end, she raised over eight hundred pounds. We also started the process of registering the charity which would be named Marley's Aart Foundation. This was a tedious process and after filling all the forms and getting all the signatures from trustees and witnesses, I submitted the application on the website only to be advised two weeks later that the application did not qualify as the starting funds were below five thousand pounds. I had somehow missed this important point that in order to register the charity, then, it should have generated an income of five thousand pounds. It was a setback but did not stop us from moving forward to opening the charity account, creating the website, and starting the planning for the fundraising walk in December 2021.

The next obstacle was creating the JustGiving account. I wanted to create an account in the charity's name, but it was not possible as we were missing the elusive charity registration number from the charity commission because the charity was not yet registered. After trying different avenues, the best which was open to us was doing a crowd funding page for the fundraising walk. At this time, I had also been advised it would be good to be recognised by the Inland Revenue, so I had to fill more forms, read through lots of information on the internet to get the recognition from Her

Majesty's Revenue and Customs (HMRC). In December, just after the first Marley's 8KM Memory Walk, we received the confirmation letter from the HMRC that the foundation was now a recognised charity for Inland Revenue purposes. There was still the charity registration to do but this needed to be done once we had raised five thousand pounds or more from the fundraising walk which by this time, we had agreed to name Marley's 8KM Memory Walk. We successfully achieved the minimum amount to register the charity. This was a key milestone as it meant we had met a key criterion for the application for the registration. In July 2022, after a lot of backwards and forwards with the case worker at the charity commission, Marley's Aart Foundation was registered as a charity in England and Wales. This was a victorious day for us as trustees. We had spent hours in preparation, meetings and of course reading and signing documents to ensure that we understood and were aligned on how we should run the charity and meet the needs of its objectives. I was very happy we had done this by ourselves without paying for services to provide guidance and direction on how to register a charity as all the money saved could go towards helping young people.

Whilst we were setting up the charity and also preparing for the fundraising walk, I also started having meetings with Marley's secondary school. I wanted Marley's Aart Foundation to play some part in making school life more comfortable and bearable for children who were transferring from the primary school to secondary school. The initial plan was to fund buddy benches inscribed with Marley's name which would be put in the playground where the new intake of year seven children aged 11–12 could connect and make new friends. I did not want other children to go through what Marley had endured throughout his secondary school life. It was a great day when we succeeded in having the first one installed at Queensbury Academy in Dunstable UK in October 2021.

I mentioned earlier that I wanted Trevor and Nathan to be involved in the charity. Whilst I had the need to channel my pain and loss in this way, for Trevor it was different. He preferred to support without being a trustee of the charity. Nathan on the other hand, is a co-founder and a trustee. At first, he found it difficult to understand where he fitted in apart from being Marley's brother. He did not want to be involved just because Marley was his brother. He found his calling when we realised that we needed a website for the public to visit and understand what Marley's Aart Foundation is about. He got a lead from one of my colleagues and from that he created the website. It was not straight forward but he kept at it until the website was created and functional, which you can check out at www.marleysaartfoundation.com He soon realised that his role is being the creative trustee as he created the Instagram page for the foundation and manages it. He also successfully identified the company who would produce the vests worn for Marley's 8KM Memory Walk all over the world.

Chapter Six

Birthdays and Anniversaries – Mum's View

Some of the hardest things to accept after you lose someone are the birthdays and anniversaries that are celebrated together. Every anniversary becomes a reminder of the difference between now and how it was before. The first Christmas was very difficult. We had to start a new tradition with the three of us and after navigating it, we felt very proud of ourselves that we would be able to face any of the others to come. Well, that was what I thought. New Year was always low key, so I did not expect it to be emotional. Sometimes it's what you don't expect that really hits you.

The first of these birthdays was Nathan's in February. I was not looking forward to it because I did not know how any of us would feel. It so happened that one of my nieces was getting married on the same day in Sierra Leone. Although I could not be there in person, I planned to join virtually since they had catered for family and friends who could not physically be there because the pandemic was still in force and travelling was not back to normal. Whilst Nathan's birthday was not a significant milestone like the previous year, I still wanted us to make it special. I decided we would bring Marley into it by watching the video recordings we had done when we went on holiday. I also wanted Nathan to transfer these videos to my phone and then to my laptop, so I had back-up in case anything went wrong with my phone. I soon realised that these were precious memories which I did not want to lose, hence the backups.

Trevor and Nathan were not keen on reliving these memories as they thought it would be too emotional. I disagreed of course and they agreed to humour me. After watching a few of the ones we took in Barbados about fourteen years ago, they soon got into it and realised that it was not as emotional as they had first thought. The videos took us back to memories when we had had a good time with Marley, what they were into as children and also some petty sibling squabbles which made us laugh. It was refreshing to relive those moments and we got lost in memory lane. Even though Trevor had been reluctant he soon got into it as he was the one who had done most of the recording. We laughed at the recordings I had done, as you could easily tell the difference because mine were all over the place.

The day was progressing nicely, and we felt that Marley was with us even though not physically. We could hear his four-year-old voice in the videos taken in Barbados and then his eleven-year-old voice in the videos taken in Florida. Later we ordered a takeaway from MacDonald's. I ordered what Marley would usually order, a Big Mac, although I stuck with a single rather than a double, which was his favourite. After the meal, which was a lot and I would not make a habit of ordering on a regular basis, I connected on zoom with family and friends for my niece's wedding. It was great to be part of it even though it was virtual, and it also helped to make Nathan's birthday memorable for all the right reasons.

The next celebration was Mother's Day, and I was dreading it as whilst I was preparing myself for an emotional breakdown it might turn out to be just an ordinary day. It was not that Marley was in the habit of doing something special on Mother's Day for me, it was more that he would not be there.

34

I need not have worried as it turned out to be a very good day. There was an inspiring message from my Pastors in the church service, there were cards from unexpected sources and also Nathan and Trevor went out of their way to make it special. I had Marley's card from 2020, which I would always treasure so that came out from the drawer and was placed with the others. Nathan kept asking me how I was and making sure that I was not feeling too sad. When I look back on that day it definitely went better than I expected.

I was feeling stronger. We were all feeling stronger. We had navigated a birthday, Mother's Day and also Easter with no setbacks. The next milestone in my opinion was Trevor's birthday in July. I thought if Nathan's birthday had gone alright, then why not the same for Trevor. You can imagine how blindsided I was when the month of June turned up and I fell apart. I was not expecting it. Every eleventh day of the month I had been lighting a candle for Marley, posting messages on my WhatsApp status to mark the day. I was also putting flowers on his grave at the cemetery, either the weekend before the eleventh or the weekend after. This was my new routine; I was expecting June to be no different. When I woke up on Saturday 5 June it felt like any other Saturday. I had my quiet time with the Lord followed by prayer time with my close family friend who had been supporting me since Marley passed. After this it was a day to deep clean the house and as usual, I put on gospel songs on my iPad connected to a speaker and I was singing and praising as I did the cleaning when suddenly it dawned on me that on this day, six months ago, was the last time the four of us had cleaned the house as a family of four.

I was suddenly hit with this overwhelming sadness. It was as if I was back in December, the last Saturday Marley was with us. Everything we had done that day, including the argument Marley and I had had when I told him to spend some of his birthday money on clothes that he needed and not on junk food. I was thinking to myself, *how did I miss this?* I checked the calendar in the kitchen and then realised that the month of June had the exact dates and day as December 2020, except that December had 31 days whilst June had 30 days. I had been told by someone that when the eleventh fell on the exact day when the event happened, it would be tough, so I had checked earlier in the year and knew that the 11 June would be on a Friday. But this was where I stopped. It did not occur to me that for the eleventh to be a Friday all the days leading before that date and after would be exactly the same as December. I was prepared in my mind for Friday the 11 June but not for the days before or the days after. What made it worse was having the knowledge of what actions Marley was putting in place without knowing the impact this would have on us for the rest of our lives. Also knowing that the 5 December was when he had made a significant purchase.

I continued cleaning but I was crying silently until I got a phone call from another good friend. She was calling to check on me and the moment she asked how I was, I fell apart and started sobbing. She immediately thought the worst had happened as it was only six months ago; I was giving her devastating news. Her immediate assumption was that something terrible had happened. She started praying but at the same time asking me what was wrong. "Is Trevor, okay?" she asked. "What about Nathan?" she continued to question me. I continued to cry, but informed her they were both fine, only struggling to come to terms with our loss and the dates that would prove to be a constant reminder. She breathed a sigh of relief that nothing terrible had happened and continued to pray with me. After praying for me she asked if I would like to go grocery shopping with her when I had finished cleaning. I was not too sure about it as I just wanted to be left alone. Sometimes it is good to be left alone but other times it is best if you are surrounded by others who care for you. On this occasion I wanted to be left alone but I would be open to company later. We agreed that she would stop by later on her way to the supermarket and if I was up to it, I would go with her.

I needed the space to think and grieve, let out some of the pain and hurt as I was feeling that piercing pain in my chest all over again and I knew I could not just bottle it up. Trevor and Nathan had noticed that I was crying and the difference in our process made itself very clear again. They were both asking why I was crying. I wanted to scream and shout, "Really, you don't know that today, exactly six months ago, Marley was ordering a rope to end his life. How could you ask me why I am crying. Where have you been the last six months?" What I now realise is the capacity I have to store and recall all these details is a unique quality I have and they don't.

I did not scream or shout but something in my expression must have caused something to click in their brains, as Nathan immediately said, "It's Marley you are thinking of."

I nodded as I could not say anything. He gave me a hug. We had earlier intended to go over to visit the family, but I was not in the mood to face anyone outside of *our* family. Nathan was torn between going with his dad and staying with me. I was feeling much more composed by this time and told them I would be alright. It would be good for me to be by myself. They were reluctant but, in the end, they left me alone. I sat outside in the garden and listened to music. I had discovered CeCe Winans' album around this time and I had it on loop whilst I relived 5 December 2020. The song "Believe for It" (written by CeCe Winans, Dwan Hill, Kylie Lee and Mitch Wong) was my favourite:

> You are the way when there seems to be no way,
> We trust in You God, You have the final say."
> Move the immovable
> Break the unbreakable
> God, we believe
> God, we believe for it

An hour or so later, I was feeling better.

Another friend called me, and we chatted for about an hour or so. She had lost her dad and her brother within days apart. We encouraged each other and I felt I needed a change of scenery and the offer from my friend Jacqueline to go grocery shopping would be a welcome change. Whilst my faith in God is very strong, I know I could not have survived without my army of friends and family. There was always someone there if I needed to talk or if I needed someone to go somewhere. Later I would check the calendar for the coming years to identify what other months had dates and days similar to December 2020. I wanted to be prepared. The rest of June was not as devastating. Although each day leading to the eleventh was playing vividly in my mind, I was more prepared after Saturday 5 June.

Trevor's birthday came round in July, and we had a quiet day. Trevor is not one to make any fuss, or so he kept telling me. I know that if we did not recognise the day he would feel put out. I know this from the odd comments he drops now and again. We had a nice meal and gave him presents. He got two fish for the outside fishpond, and it kept him busy acclimatising them to their new surroundings and a new family of fish.

September was not far away, and it would be my birthday. It was the first time I had not been looking forward to it. Whilst Trevor was not a big fan of celebrating his birthday, I was the opposite. I always planned to do something nice even if it was just taking the day off from work so I could talk to friends and family far and wide. This year I did not know how I would feel on the day. I wanted to make a conscious effort to have a good day and to start creating new memories. My birthday was on a Thursday and I would be having tea with two ladies from my church on the Friday, the day after my birthday. This was definitely something to look forward to. I had taken the Thursday and the Friday off work so I could have a long weekend break. I thought because I had been expecting my birthday to be difficult, I had subconsciously been preparing myself.

I felt no different on the morning of my birthday. Trevor and Nathan made sure that I did not feel emotional. From the morning when I got up until I went to bed there were calls and texts and friends stopping by with gifts and flowers and cards and cakes. Trevor had an urgent family matter that he needed to attend to, and although he was reluctant to leave us alone, I encouraged him to go and assured him that Nathan and I would be fine. Besides, we had our friends who would either visit or call to speak with me.

The day and days after were memorable. I received lots of texts and calls of good wishes and blessings from all over the world. Besides the flowers, cakes, gifts and cards from friends and family there were invites for dinners and lunches. I really felt cared for and continued to thank everyone who did not give me a moment to be sad, especially Nathan. Don't get me wrong, I did think of Marley as there is not a day that goes by without me thinking of him. He would be forever ingrained in my thoughts.

Our wedding anniversary which followed in October was uneventful. After previous birthday celebrations I was not expecting any unexpected triggers to make me emotional. My sadness was borne out of the change in weather and the seasons as we were now in autumn and approaching winter. The days were shorter and the nights longer and I was not looking forward to it. Added to this I had all the timeline imprinted in my mind of the intense research he was doing around this time in 2020. I realised that I would have to get used to this time of the year for different reasons. Before, it was just the fact that it got quite cold and dark; now there was the added element of Marley not being here.

Chapter Seven

Getting Out There – Mum's View

Although I had previously told the family that we would not be doing anymore vacations when we had come back from Sierra Leone after all the stress I had gone through, it did not extend to short breaks. After the last seven months and the lockdowns we had endured, I was keen to go away somewhere; anywhere within the UK was good as I could not contend with all the bureaucracy of travelling abroad. I knew this would not be an easy subject to broach with Trevor and Nathan, and as much as they would have liked a change of scenery, there were other things to think about. How would it feel stepping out as a family of three instead of the usual four? *I can tell you. It is hard.* No sugarcoating it, but life had to go on. As much as Trevor and Nathan did not want to do it, I strongly felt that we needed it. We had been cocooned in our home for a long time and we needed a change of scenery. I knew I would have my work cut out as Trevor was not keen on driving far.

I started by researching where we could go that would be far enough but would be manageable to drive to and back within the day. At this time I was not thinking of an overnight stay as I thought it would be a hard sell with Trevor. I thought a zoo would be good. We enjoyed going to the zoo when the children were younger so that could be a good place to start. I also thought somewhere located by the seaside would be good as we all loved it when we had gone on beach holidays, although it is not the same in England. With these two things in mind, I started doing my research on the internet. Not long after I started searching, I came across Africa Live Zoological Reserve in Lowestoft, Suffolk. It was over a two-hour drive. We could go the scenic route, stop on the way and back, which would take about a five-hour round trip. I told Trevor about it, and he thought it would be better if we stayed overnight instead of doing the round trip on the same day. I was pleasantly surprised when he said to do overnight. This was perfect as it meant we could visit more places. I also shared with Nathan how he felt about visiting the zoo I had identified and staying overnight. He was also fine with it, especially since he had been confined to the house the week before we went due to catching the coronavirus.

I decided to do more research on what other places we could visit, hotels we could stay at and restaurants where we could eat. This was great. I had something to plan: what we needed to take with us, the route we needed to take, when to leave and what we were able to take with us. After getting the tickets for the zoo I also got tickets for Sea Life in Great Yarmouth as I had decided we would stay at a hotel in Great Yarmouth so we could take a walk by the seaside. If we were going to see the animals at the zoo on land it made sense also to see the creatures in the water. After I had booked everything, I shared it with Nathan. He got excited as it awakened his childhood memories of family outings of going to Whipsnade Zoo.

On the morning of our trip to the zoo, we got up early so we could get to our first destination in good time. It was only an overnight stay, but I had packed a lot of things. I was not taking any chances. I had packed everything from painkillers to beddings, from cutleries to mugs, as I was not too sure about the hotel we were staying at. Most hotels in Great Yarmouth were booked up and there were hardly any rooms available in a good location by the seafront. Trevor and Nathan were wondering why I had so many bags but later on they would thank me for having the insight to take some of the things which they were making fun of.

When we set off it was a nice day. The outward journey was good as we followed the Satnav and soon, we were picking up signs for the zoo. On the way, we drove past some young women who had been desperate for the bathroom, and it was obvious that they could not find one as they were crouched on the side of the road. It amused us that this was something that was common to us all: *when you've got to go, you've got to go*. They were desperate for the bathroom. It's one of the reasons why Trevor does not like doing long journeys as there are not many places where you can stop to use the toilet, especially if it's not on the motorway. Maybe investing in a portable toilet is something one should consider for long journeys.

Not too long after, we arrived at the zoo, and it turned out to be a lovely day. The zoo was not too full, and we could find a parking space and move around easily. We were able to catch some of the feeding times for the animals and listen to some of the background stories. What really amused us was the lions. There were about five of them and all they did whilst we were there was sleep. They are supposed to be the "Kings of the Jungle", yet they were more "Sleep of the Jungle". They would get up, move a couple of feet forward and drop back to the grass like a sack of potatoes. Nathan was able to do a short clip of one of the lions doing just that. It was simple but it was fun. My favourite thing to do was watch the meerkats; there were loads of them. In real life they appeared so much smaller than watching them on TV. It was great seeing how they chased each other, how carefree they were. Although Marley crossed my mind a few times whilst we were at the zoo and we did say that he would have enjoyed it, we were not sad or emotional. It takes a lot of courage and determination to do something for the first time without a loved one who has passed but when you do it, it feels very freeing.

When we left the zoo, we drove to the hotel. It should have taken us twenty minutes but took about an hour because of road works and diversions. The hotel was worse than I had expected but there was nothing we could do about it. We checked in and settled into our room. It was a suite to sleep up to four people. I soon realised once we got into the suite that my bedding would be needed as well as the cutlery and mugs. Trevor and Nathan assured me that it was only for one night and we could manage. We relaxed a bit then we stepped out for dinner. I had booked a restaurant with high ratings for good fish. We found our way there and then we were faced for the first time with being seated at a table for four when there were now only three of us. Trevor and I usually sat facing Nathan and Marley. For the first time we had an empty chair in front of us and it was hard for all of us but more so for me. Although the last dinner we had at a restaurant with Marley was for Nathan's twenty-first birthday and he was miserable, I would rather have had him there with us sulking or miserable than not at all. That may sound selfish, but it was hard knowing that he would never share another dinner with us in this life. The meal was lovely, the atmosphere was good, but it did bring home for me that Marley was no longer with us.

After dinner we walked back to the hotel and that night I dreamt about Marley. He was happy in the dream which is how he is when I have dreams of him. I believe it is one of the ways God reassures me that Marley is fine, as every dream I have had of him he has been happy and, in the dream, we would have a wonderful time together to the extent that when I woke up, I am filled with joy. I had not felt sad. I shared with Trevor and Nathan what I had dreamt, and they said it was his way of comforting me after being sad at dinner. We went for a walk by the beach before going to the Sea Life Centre. We saw penguins and different types of sea creatures at the centre before making our way home. Our journey back was not as uneventful as we missed our turning on the motorway and drove for about ten minutes on the new road which the Satnav could not pick up because it was not up to date. It added an additional thirty minutes to our journey home. Trevor was not amused, and I knew it would take a lot of convincing to get him to go on another long journey. That would be a battle for another day.

A few weeks after our overnight stay in Great Yarmouth, Trevor and I had an invitation to a sixtieth birthday party with an overnight stay. There is one thing I have accepted over the years being married to Trevor is that he is a homebody. If he had his way, he would not go anywhere because his favourite pastime is chilling at home. When I broached the subject of going to this birthday celebration his first reaction was to reject it because he was not in a party mood, and he did not think he would feel like it on the day. If there is one thing, I have learnt in the last eight months is to be persistent. There was no way I would let him dwell on how he was feeling and not try to get him out of that funk. It was for this reason that since we lost Marley, I always found a project around the house for him to get his teeth into because his way of showing that he cares is by fixing things and taking care of any DIY project especially since he retired. For Nathan it was all about exercise, going to the gym was his passion so when he did not go for two to three days, I knew he was in a funk, especially if he was not sick. I was constantly watching over the two of them to ensure that they were looking after their mental health. By no means did I think we were over what had happened in December 2020, even though we were going through life almost as normal.

After some convincing from both Nathan and me, Trevor agreed to go to the party. Nathan was happy to have the house to himself for the first time since Marley passed. Whilst I had some misgivings about leaving him by himself overnight, he was keen to see the back of us and could not wait for us to drive off. Some of my concerns were, what if he found it hard to be on his own in the house by himself? What if he became lonely and sad? I sometimes forget that he is an adult. As a mum, you tend to worry about everything. I am sure I am not the only one.

The party was lovely. We were joined by two other lovely couples, one who we knew and the other we got to know during the course of the evening. Whilst I enjoyed myself, thoughts of Marley were not far off. As I remembered just four years ago when I was celebrating a significant birthday with family and friends with no inkling that three years later, I would be heartbroken with the loss of Marley. Although Trevor had been reluctant to go, he enjoyed himself and did not take up the offer to retire to the hotel room if it got too much for him. He stayed and partied until the music was turned off at midnight. Over the years I have learnt that if there is an option to stay overnight in the hotel it is easier to convince him to go to an event. Knowing that there is a room within an arm's length that he could retire to if things got too much for him, takes away whatever reservations he might have had of attending the event. Nathan also had a good night. He had invited a few of his friends over for drinks so he had company.

Not long after, we received another invitation to my cousin's fiftieth birthday in Kent. It was also being held at a hotel with the option of staying overnight. On this occasion I could not convince Trevor to go with me. The fact that it was in November and most days were similar to 11 December did not help. I was a bit concerned that he would be on his own as around this time Nathan was working weekends and also late hours. On the morning when I was leaving, Trevor said, "I am going to be on my own when Nathan goes to work later." He is not one to make a fuss, but I read between the lines, the words which he had left unsaid. It was the first time that he would be on his own for that length of time and he would be lonely. It's not easy trying to second guess what was going through his mind but on this occasion, it was very clear.

After he dropped me off at the train station, I texted two of his friends to pop round and see him as he would be on his own during the day. Fortunately, one of them could make it even though it was short notice. Trevor, like most men find it difficult to reach out for help even when they need it. I really thank God for friends who can be there for us at the drop of a hat. Similar to the other birthday celebrations, I realised that as much as I could enjoy myself to a certain extent, Marley and the similarity to my celebrations brought back memories. Still, it was good to get out there as I reconnected with family from America who I had not seen since the event of December 2020. I was able to talk about that day without tears which was a successful milestone in itself.

Before the pandemic, I used to do business travels two to three times a month. Since February 2020, I had not travelled and in October 2021, I had to travel to Sweden for business. It would be the first time I had travelled outside of the UK and stayed away from home since Marley had passed. I was not looking forward to it because I did not know how I would feel but until you try something you will never know. As we took steps forward in living without Marley, there would be things we would have to do, even if our natural instincts were to avoid it. I focused on the positive aspects of my travel: I would be seeing, and meeting team members based in Stockholm, Sweden, for the first time in real life as they had joined the team during lockdown. I had only met them on video calls. I was not travelling alone as I had a friend and colleague who was also based in the UK, and we would be travelling together so I had someone to keep me distracted.

When I look back at my trip, I am glad I did it as the other opportunity for travel would have been in December and I really did not want to travel at that time. The trip was successful, and I realised I could do it. There were moments when I felt sad, for example, when I met my previous manager who had been so supportive to me when Marley had passed, and also meeting other friends and colleagues for the first time since December. It was emotional, however, good to get that first meeting out of the way. Even though they were not there, I could tell that they shared some of the pain and loss I had experienced and was still experiencing. I had also used the opportunity to take the vests we would wear for Marley's 8KM Memory Walk with me.

Chapter Eight

Emotional Triggers – Mum's View

In the early days, one of the things we feared as a family was coming across people who had no clue that Marley was no longer with us. We had tried as best as we could to inform everyone who was close to us and those who were not so close. I had gone through my contacts to ensure that most people who knew him and us had been informed. Whilst going through my contacts I realised that there were still some friends whom I had missed because we had not been in contact with them in the last two years or so. These people would have no idea. I was in two minds whether to reach out to them or not as I thought if there had not been any contact for that length of time, then it was likely that that would continue. So, I was a bit hesitant. I was forced to act when Trevor had an incident with someone who used to be close to us whilst the children were growing up.

Trevor had gone to our local shop and whilst he was there, he came across the mother of one of Nathan and Marley's childhood friend who we have had no contact with for over fifteen years. Trevor was not planning to say hello as he thought she would not recognise him. But even when you do not see someone for a long time – whether or not there have been physical changes – you still recognise one another. We think we can get away with not making eye contact. In most cases if we can identify the person, of course they will recognise us too. In this instance Trevor thought he could avoid eye contact and not have to make small talk. How wrong he was. He was soon accosted by this woman, with the question we have now come to dread, "How are the boys? They must be quite grown men now," she continued without noticing that Trevor had not yet responded to the first question or the tension this question had created.

After what felt like a long time but only a few minutes in reality, she noticed that Trevor had not said anything. So, she went on to say, "You are Nathan and Marley's dad, right?"

Trevor answered, "Yes, I am, although Marley is no longer with us." Trevor's response was not what she was expecting, and she became very emotional in the shop, which put Trevor in an uncomfortable position. I don't know about other people but when I am going through a painful situation and I am trying to be strong and I see someone else being emotional because of something that has happened to me it creates a trigger, it takes me back to that pain and loss. The woman was in tears and very visibly upset. It's not the answer you expect when you ask someone how their children are doing. The worst still was yet to come, the next dreaded question was "what did he die of"? Or how did he die? For the person asking the question, it is normal that you follow up with what took that person's life, usually sickness or an accident that the person had no control over. It is a tough question for the receiver as it triggers the pain and loss. I never knew how difficult those questions were until I was the receiver and, in a situation where I didn't want to answer. Trevor told her that Marley had ended his life and because she could not control her emotions, she was now attracting the attention of other shoppers. Trevor quickly said his goodbyes whilst she was still enquiring about me and promising to visit. It was difficult for Trevor. He did not want to share about Marley, and he was neither prepared to be asked those questions nor the impact his answers would have on the receiver. This incident definitely put us on our guard.

Due to the pandemic and lockdown, I had not been to the church building for service for a long time and though I joined the online church events, I had a choice of using video or just audio. My first time back to the church building was going to be emotional so I asked Nathan and Trevor to go with me. Nathan agreed but Trevor thought it would be too emotional for him. I decided to do this the Sunday before my birthday. I prayed that everyone I would meet already knew that Marley passed so that I would not have to deal with questions which could trigger me emotionally. Although it was a beautiful service, I was very emotional for other reasons. This was the church where Marley was dedicated to God as a baby, attended Sunday school, and was a regular at the front as one of the children from Sunday school singing or part of a presentation. He was also Joseph in the nativity over the years, and it was the same church where we had held the farewell service for him ten months ago. It was bound to be emotional. The good thing was, Nathan was with me, and I got a lot of comfort from that. Whilst it was tough, I did not let it put me off going to the physical building as I thought the more, I went, the less painful it would be and this would become part of the new normal.

I purposed in my heart to go to Sunday service in the physical church once every month until I felt more comfortable and could go more often. I have read of other people finding it hard to go to church after losing someone, so I knew I was not alone in my feelings. It's not all cases it's because they are angry with God but because you meet people who forces you to face your loss head on because of something they say or do without knowing how emotionally fragile you are, even though it might be years after your loss. I must say that there has been only one occasion when someone has asked about Marley since I started going back to church. "How are the boys doing?" she had asked. On this occasion I decided not to go into details and just said that the boys were fine. She had wanted to continue on that topic, but I was very quick to change the focus from me to hers. Technically, I believe Marley is doing great where he is now. What I omitted to say is that he is no longer in his physical body but his spirit lives on.

Don't get me wrong, not everyone would get the memo of what happened that the family of four is now a family of three or that the person who is no longer with us left under traumatic circumstances. What is needed in these situations is some sensitivity. I suggest letting the person volunteer the information, if they feel comfortable doing so. Don't fire one question after the other to them.

There are other triggers which we would not be able to control. I had created a family WhatsApp group some years ago when I was travelling a lot and needed to send just one message to everyone instead of sending three. When Marley passed it was a silent agreement that we would not take him off the group, and we would keep the same profile picture of the four of us. You can imagine my surprise when ten months later I saw on my phone on the group chat, "Marley left". I was shocked. I thought Trevor or Nathan had taken him off the group. They had both got similar messages and were wondering if I had taken him off the group chat. We realised that none of us had done so and it must have been initiated by the owners of WhatsApp. It made me emotional as I was not expecting it and it also brought afresh the fact that he had left us, another unwanted reminder.

There was also the incident with the death certificate. I had delegated the task of getting the death certificate to Trevor as the interim certificate had caused me a lot of emotional stress. He had contacted the registry for births and deaths and paid the required fee. Three weeks later, what we thought was the certificate arrived, it took Trevor a few minutes to open the envelope as he knew what the contents were. After psyching himself to open it, it turned out that it was not ours. The registration office had sent us three certificates belonging to someone else. It was difficult for him to do it the first time and he had to do it again. Due to this error, he had to call them again and also to post the ones which another family was expecting but not received because they had had been sent to us, the wrong address. It seemed like something small, but these small things cause a lot of unwanted stress. On the second attempt the registration office got it right. When we got it out of the envelope, and you could see in black and white that Marley was gone, the impact on us was tough.

One of the things that really causes a trigger for me is the dates, which immediately bring Marley to the forefront of my mind. I am always thinking of what was happening around that time, not having the knowledge that the time with Marley was coming to an end. You hear people say what they would do if they knew their time on earth was coming to an end, but in this situation, I wonder what I would have done differently. Thinking about it but not wanting to dwell on it as that was the first advice we were given on that fateful day, there are definitely some things I would have done more of and some things I would have done less of. I would have listened more, spent more time with Marley than the "me time" I craved after a busy day at work. I would not have focused on the little things like leaving the water bottle empty in the fridge or taking the last tissue from the tissue box and leaving the empty box for someone else to put in the bin. I would definitely not have insisted that he spent his birthday money on the clothes that he did not live to enjoy.

In September 2021 Emma Raducanu, the British tennis player was making headlines in the news after becoming Britain's first female Grand Slam champion since 1977 for winning the US Open. I remember waking up that morning after she had won the final and being very happy for her and her parents, but then becoming very low in my spirit when it dawned on me that she was born the same year as Marley, less than a month before Marley was born. At the time she won the US Open she was eighteen, the same age as Marley was. I started thinking of all the stuff Marley could have achieved and what I had missed out on. Honestly, I could not understand why I was in pieces, crying my eyes out of what could have been, but there I was, reliving all the stuff that I thought I had cried out of my system. I must have cried for over thirty minutes before I felt better. Fortunately, I was alone downstairs so neither Nathan nor Trevor could hear me. After this incident I learnt that I could never prepare myself for every situation or event which could trigger off feelings of emotion. I had to depend on God. He is the one who gives me strength to face life head on as the Bible says, "Do not fear [anything], for I am with you; Do not be afraid, for I am your God. I will strengthen you, be assured I will help you; I will certainly take hold of you with My righteous right hand [a hand of justice, of power, of victory, of salvation].

With Nathan it's usually when he hears that someone else ended their life, especially when there is a sibling involved who has had to experience similar emotions to what he has gone through. This usually happens when he watches the news or social media. There was an occasion when he felt really sad because he was thinking that he would be on his own when Trevor and I passed. I listed all his numerous cousins in England, Sierra Leone and other countries. I assured him that he would be fine, especially if he goes on to have his own family. He has some really good friends who have continued to support him.

Chapter Nine

Overcoming Fear – Mum's View

The finality of death and the unknown is scary for all of us. When you die, how you die are some of the things that concern us. For some of us we are fearful of leaving others behind, even though we would not be around, the caretaker in us would worry about how the people we would leave behind would cope without us. For others they are fearful of losing the ones who are close to them as they could not imagine life without those people who they are close to. When someone dies in the family, this fear becomes even more real, especially when it was not expected. On the other hand, when someone is sick and the doctors give you a prognosis, if the prognosis is not good, even though you don't want to lose that person, you know that eventually they will pass and leave you and so you are forced to begin the grieving process whilst the loved one is still alive. This was what I experienced when I lost my mum but that is a story for another day.

Losing Marley in the way that we did caused me to be fearful of losing anyone else. It was all about the unexpected, not being in control of the future. It creates a fear that has no factual grounds apart from what has happened, the possibility that it could happen again gets a hold of you and becomes this fear that you cannot shake off. I know that this fear was not from God, but I had been hit hard by the unexpected. I was thinking we were now a family of three and if anything happens to any of us our family could be halved. You can imagine how I felt when Nathan suddenly started getting vertigo out of nowhere. The first episode was in February after Marley passed in December. He was so sick; he could not eat anything without throwing up. He had to be horizontal or he felt that everything was spinning around him. It was very worrying. He could only get telephone appointments with the doctor due to the pandemic and each medication prescribed was not effective. He started doing his own research on the internet and discovered some exercises which could help. After three to four days, he felt better. I had reached everyone who could pray to lift him up in prayer. When he got better, we thought that was the end of it. But it wasn't. A few months later in May, he was confined to his bed again with the same thing. The difference this time was that he knew it was coming as he started feeling the same way he had felt the last time before he was sick and confined to his bed.

A few days later he got better only for him to be sick again. We could not understand what was causing it. The doctors at the surgery could not see him physically and were making a diagnosis based on phone appointments, which was frustrating and unhelpful. He had started looking for employment but because of being handicapped by the vertigo it made him reluctant to get a job. How could he start working and then take time off for sickness? When he felt better, I booked the three of us for a private health check. I wanted to get to the bottom of this.

In September we had the health check and the results came back three weeks later. We were all fine, nothing was wrong, however, mid-October he had another episode. We were slowly accepting that this was something that he may have to live with but in my heart, I was not accepting it. When he recovered, I encouraged him to look for the jobs that he had been interested in and for him to apply as not working was causing him to be down. He succeeded and in November he started working again. He had only been working for a week when he came home rushing to the bathroom because he was sick. I thought enough is enough. When he got into his bed, I said I was going to pray for him. I had prayed before but nothing like this. I was angry, very angry and I thought to myself, *I have to put a stop to this so help me God.* I told him we were not going to accept vertigo popping on and off and stopping him from living a normal life. I remember putting my hands on his head and prayed, commanding the vertigo and everything associated with it to go in Jesus' name. I also asked for wisdom and knowledge to know what the root cause was for the vertigo so that Nathan could address it. Afterwards I said to him, "You need to stop eating tuna." In October he had a lot of tuna and pasta. It was his favourite comfort food. I told him not to eat any more of it for the rest of the year.

He looked at me and said, "How could you just pray like that?"

"What do you mean?" I asked. It was not the first time he had heard me praying so I was curious to hear what his reply was.

"The words just flow from you, without you mumbling or thinking. It seems so natural," he responded.

"It's the Holy Spirit in me," I said. As the Bible says, "But you will receive power and ability when the Holy Spirit comes upon you; and you will be My witnesses [to tell people about Me] both in Jerusalem and in all Judea, and Samaria, and even to the ends of the earth." (Act 1:8 AMP) "You need to trust God now for your healing and stop eating tuna."

He just smiled and said, "We will see."

As I write, it's been ten months since he had that episode in November. He actually admitted that he has never felt better. He has not eaten tuna and he is feeling great. That incident caused me to trust God even more for my family. I hold on to what The Bible says, "No temptation has overtaken you except what is common to mankind. And God is faithful; he would not let you be tempted beyond what you could bear" (1 Corinthians10:13 AMP). I have to trust God; he cares for me and if anything happens, he allowed it for a reason. I am constantly talking to him about Marley and asking if there could be another way, but each time it's almost as if it's an audible voice saying to me, "it was the only option that you would be able to bear". I don't think I am special or closer to God than the next person, but I slowly started to believe that we are all on this earth for a purpose and we will be here for as long as we have been purposed.

In our human thinking we put time into two boxes; a longer period of time and a shorter period of time, but God is timeless and we might say that Marley had a short life, but he had served his purpose. I am still here because there is more God has purposed for me to do and you are still here because there is still a purpose you need to achieve. When I focus on this thinking it really helps me to overcome the fear of losing someone. If God could not hold back His Son, Jesus, then who am I to question God on the timing of when Marley left us. This is not to say that it does not sometimes cloud my Godly thinking especially when I feel the loss and pain of losing someone. I have to ask myself, why would I become fearful of losing someone else in the family? God is in control and we are all here for a purpose.

Chapter Ten

A Beautiful Day – Mum's View

The first anniversary of Marley's passing was fast approaching and as a family there were different emotions we were experiencing as December approached. First and foremost was the first birthday without him and what that would look like. I had decided earlier on that there would not be a memorial service as the focus in December would not be on his passing. I was more focused on the day he had been born to us, which would always be special. It made sense that the first official event to raise funds collectively as trustees would be a memory walk on the Saturday closest to his birth date, Saturday 4 December 2021. The Saturday after what would have been Marley's nineteenth birthday, we had the first Marley's 8KM Memory Walk to raise funds for Marley's Aart Foundation.

A lot of planning had gone into making this day special. Time had been spent choosing the route for the walk. It needed to be the route which Marley had frequented, therefore the route leading to his secondary school, the bike shop Decathlon and his first school where he had such happy memories were also included. Once it was clear what landmarks needed to be included, it was important that we did a test walk to get an idea of how long it would take and that the walk would be about five miles, which is just over eight kilometers. On the day I did this with one of the trustees, it was a clear day. Trevor dropped us off at the starting point which was Marley's secondary school, and we walked through the town centre going past most of the places which he used to frequent including part of the route he used to do for his paper round with the end point being his first school.

I had contacted both schools to inform them of our intentions to use one or the other as our starting and end point. I did not expect that both schools would want to play some part in it. The secondary school wanted a few of the teachers to join and the primary school wanted to serve us refreshments at the end of the walk. I was really touched. I had a meeting with the head teacher of St Christopher's Academy before the walk. I took Nathan with me and as we walked, we relived some of the childhood memories when I would drop them off at school (which did not happen very often as they had their auntie who was staying with us at the time to take them to school). As we were walking, I looked ahead of me and noticed a boy who looked exactly like a young Marley wearing the St Christopher's uniform approaching us. It was like being taken back in time to all those years ago when Marley attended the school. I looked at Nathan thinking I was probably looking for Marley in every boy with some similarity but then Nathan looked at me and said, "Do you see what I see?"

"Are you looking at the young boy walking towards us?" I said.

"Yes, I am," he said.

We both agreed he looked so much like a younger Marley. I was shocked that he had seen the same resemblance that I had seen. It was almost like a sign that we were doing the right thing. When the boy got closer, we could clearly see the resemblance, but not a strong lookalike as it had appeared from afar.

It was an emotional moment when we arrived at the school, and though there were aesthetic changes on the outside, the reception was much the same as when Nathan and Marley had attended. We were introduced to the head teacher who we had never met before but soon realised we had kindred spirit. It was uncanny how she had gone through incidents recently which I could relate to. She had also spoken to a few teachers who remembered Marley and Nathan when they attended the school and they had dug up some photos of Marley which we did not have. It was a very touching visit and it also confirmed that we were making the right decision to end the walk at Marley's first school. We also accepted the hospitality being offered by the head teacher.

Towards the end of November, beginning of December, Covid cases were rising across the country, and I was happy I had encouraged supporters to walk in their location. I did not want everyone to join us in the memory walk locally as it would have been too many people. There were people in other countries also who wanted to support me and the foundation, so I encouraged anyone who was not local to walk where they were and to take videos and pictures, they would share with me afterwards. We had successfully sourced a number of vests with the foundation's name and logo, which were adapted from Marley's YouTube channel's logo by a close friend who had spent time with Nathan and Marley at a young age.

On the morning of the walk, I woke up early. I was not sure how many people would join us as I had received a few messages the days leading up to the walk that they had caught Covid and therefore could not join in. There were other unforeseen circumstances which meant not all of the trustees could join the walk either. God is so faithful because whilst I was getting these negative outward signs, I also got this innate assurance that I was doing the right thing even though there were circumstances and events which made me question if indeed it was the right thing. I really believed that this was what God wanted me to do. Also, the weather forecast for the days leading up to the walk and the day itself was not brilliant and there was a likelihood that it would be a snowy day. I was thinking that it might end up being just Nathan and me walking. How wrong I was.

I went to bed the day before the walk with all these thoughts going through my mind but God has a way of confirming again and again that He is in control. First of all, the day before the walk which would have been Marley's birthday, the scripture from Psalm 118:24, "This [day in which God has saved me] is the day which the LORD has made; Let us rejoice and be glad in it." I have a pack of cards with different scripture verses which can be changed daily. When I changed the card the scripture which was next was this one which was what I had put in Marley's eighteenth birthday card the year before. For me it was not coincidental that this same scripture was on the card I had changed that morning. On his birthday when I could have been sad it felt as if God was saying to me, *it's another day*, which He has made and just as I was saying to Marley to be happy about it, God was now saying the same thing to me. I also felt that all would be alright. I told Nathan and he did not know what to say; even though he could be skeptical about such things he realised that I was definitely getting comfort from God, as I could easily have been in tears because Marley was not with us to celebrate his birthday.

It was forecast to rain on the morning of the walk; however, I was determined that Nathan and I would still do the walk. There were some friends and family who were planning to meet us at home since I had asked Trevor to do a few drop-offs at the starting point. When Trevor dropped Nathan and me at the starting point, I was pleasantly surprised to see that about thirty to thirty-five people were already there waiting for us to start the walk. We distributed the colours to those who had not yet got the vest and we were ready to set off. As we walked the rain clouds disappeared and the sun was shining. The morning became a bright and sunny day even if it was still cold. There were people from our church as well as friends and family who joined us for the walk. I was leading the way as I was the only one who knew the exact route, since I had done the test walk.

Whilst we were walking, I was receiving text messages from supporters in different parts of the country who were also doing the five-mile walk. I was really touched when I received a picture of friends and colleagues in Stockholm, Sweden, who were also doing the walk in the snow-covered roads but with a bright shining sun. It was fantastic. In just over two hours we reached our end point, St Christopher's Academy. There was a sign at the gate welcoming Marley's Aart Foundation, which made me emotional. When we got in, I was expecting teas and coffees not a spread of cakes and biscuits and lovely food which had been prepared and laid out for us. I was really touched by the kindness and generosity of the head teacher and the school. A heartfelt thank you to all who made it a beautiful day – the first Marley's 8KM Memory Walk.

Chapter Eleven

Can December be Beautiful Again? – Mum's View

There is no doubt in our minds that the month of December would never be the same again after 2020, but how could we make it bearable, if not beautiful again? These are some of the questions which were going through our minds as we were counting down from November to December in 2021. I have already mentioned in Chapter Four – Marley's Legacy, about the foundation we set up and the first Marley's 8KM Memory Walk, which would take place every year, either Saturday before or after his birthday. There was another date, the 11 December, which was imprinted in our minds and the days after which we needed to navigate. I had hoped that the memorial headstone for the grave would be ready for installation but due to delays with raw materials, the masons at the funeral home could not get it ready in time. I had given a lot of thought to what we should do as the first anniversary of Marley's passing approached. I thought about having a memorial service or something but in the end, I wanted to keep it low key. I did not want anything that would trigger a lot of emotions of loss and grief. We were on a high from the walk which had generated support nationwide, across Europe and in Africa, and I was really happy with the support and donations from everyone which would enable Marley's Aart to make a difference in another young person's life.

The week leading to the eleventh I had a call with CHUMS, one of the organizations Marley's Aart was funding to provide Art Therapy for young people. In this call I was really encouraged that the first young person Marley's Aart was funding was a young boy aged nine and he had already had eight sessions with more to come. It was significant for me that within a year of such a traumatic loss, the pain of losing Marley was already turning into something positive. And also, because the first young person was a boy and younger made it even more significant. It is important to address any mental health issues in the very early stages as the older the young person gets, the more they are unwilling to accept help. I know this from the experience with Marley. If we had caught on at the very early stage when Marley had just transferred to his new school that he needed professional intervention, I strongly believe this would have made a difference. As around this time he was complaining about fitting in and not being able to make lasting friendships, we would have had a chance to make a difference as he would have been more receptive to it. I was feeling positive after the feedback from CHUMS regarding this young boy. It made facing the anniversary a bit more bearable.

My aunt from London had told me she would be coming to spend the day with us, being that the first anniversary would be on a Saturday. I had taken the Friday and the Monday off work as I did not want to be blindsided by the emotions that had overwhelmed me in June. We had plans to go to the cemetery to lay some flowers. My aunt was arriving earlier by train so she could go with us. I am always in a surreal state when I go to the cemetery. Part of me accepts that it is the reality, but the more time passes the more I feel like Marley went somewhere else. He seemed removed from the reality of what we experienced. It's almost as if it was somebody else. Maybe thinking like this helps me to cope with the reality, but this is how I feel when I visit his grave. I am always asking the question *why?* I am there but it is as if I am not there. Thoughts are constantly going through my head. *Am I really here visiting Marley's grave? Is this real?* It is hard to believe the reality.

When we got home from the cemetery, my aunt started preparing the usual traditional food of black-eyed beans with fried plantains and sweet potatoes, which could be eaten on their own or with white rice. Nathan had to go to work. I had encouraged him to take the time off, but he had assured me that he would be alright. Trevor was watching football whilst my aunt and I were preparing the food. I am glad that she was with us as whilst I had told friends and family that we were keeping it low key and did not want a fuss, it was good to have another female in our home. I had never navigated this road before so I did not know what I really needed. After we finished preparing the food, we were about to have dinner when a close friend stopped by. Unfortunately for her another friend of hers had lost her daughter unexpectedly and she had been on her way back home from visiting this friend. When I hear of another family, another mother going through the loss of their child, my heart bleeds for them. It is different now that I have experienced it compared to before when I had not had that experience.

Later, I dropped my aunt at the station as she returned to London. We had survived the first anniversary. *What's next?* Christmas was approaching but it did not feel like it. In previous years around the second weekend after Marley's birthday would be the time when we put up Christmas decorations both inside and outside our home.We were not in the mood, but I felt I had to shake off this feeling. We had to move forward to embracing some parts of December. Yes, it would never be the same but in my heart, I really believed that if Marley could have had a say in this, he would want us to at least put up the Christmas tree.

On Sunday 12 December, I decided that I would put up the

Christmas tree. Trevor and Nathan were opposed to it, but I knew once I had the tree up, they would come round. Trevor got me all the stuff from the loft, and I put the tree up. I found it really helpful as the mood in our home changed. It no longer felt sad and empty. All around us, the neighbours had put up some form of Christmas decorations. When coming home in the evening our house – which used to be lit up around this time of the year – was the only one in a cluster of about five houses with no Christmas lights, no indication that Christmas was round the corner. I was not yet ready to put any Christmas lights outside and maybe I will never be ready for that as we had done in the past, but I felt this was a good step forward. I also got some lights for the windows at the front of the house which included Marley's room. Marley always loved to have lights in his room so I was glad I could do it this year. Last year we were in no position to do this but this year we could. I also put in the order for some of the other food stuff we usually have for Christmas.

After all the plans I had made for Christmas, on Christmas Eve I tested positive for Covid, so Christmas day was not the same. Nathan was trying to stay away from me but he could not prepare the meal we had planned. Trevor was resigned to the fact that he, too, probably had Covid so there was no point in him isolating himself from me. By Boxing Day, all of us had Covid. It was good that we had no plans to visit with family as it would have been a disaster. Since it was just the three of us, we made the best of it. I pushed for us to prepare the food we had planned as surprisingly we had not lost our appetite. After the holidays I thought it would be good if we could do something different together the following year.

God has a way of bringing some good in a dark day. Whilst December would no longer be the same, I was pleasantly surprised when on 31 December 2021, one of my nieces who was expecting her baby between Christmas and the New Year, gave birth to a baby boy. Indeed, God could make life beautiful again as The Bible says, "To grant to those who mourn in Zion the following: To give them a turban instead of mourning, The garment of praise instead of a disheartened spirit. So, they would be called the trees of righteousness [strong and magnificent, distinguished for integrity, justice and right standing with God], The planting of the Lord, that He may be glorified" (Isaiah 61:3 AMP).

Without any prior knowledge he was given two names of significance to Marley and our family. The first of which was Benjamin after Marley's granddad and the second was Trevor's middle name, Anthony. I really felt that God was saying something unique in the situation. First significance was the extended family had been blessed with another male child and second the names were very significant because of the connection to Marley. I was so happy for my niece and her husband as this was the niece who had got married in February 2021 on the same day as Nathan's birthday. I believed that God was turning our mourning into dancing as The Bible says, "You have turned my mourning into dancing for me; You have taken off my sackcloth and clothed me with joy, that my soul may sing praise to You and not be silent. O Lord my God, I will give thanks to You forever" (Psalm 30:11-12 AMP).

Chapter Twelve

The Dark Clouds Will Get Lighter – Mum's View

If you have read my first book *Marley's Memoir: The Journey to an Irreversible Action and the Aftermath* you would already know that I'm a Christian and have a very strong faith in God. Similar to the first book I have included bible references in some of the chapters, and also lyrics from a gospel song for those who would understand the context and would draw strength from them. I hope that there would be a lot of people from other faiths or religions who would read this book, and I would like to say I could only refer to what I know and what has really been a source of strength for me and my family during this difficult time. There are also others who have no faith or religion, and I hope you will also get something out of reading this book.

It is usual after a traumatic loss in a family that as the days become weeks, the weeks become months, and months become years, that those who were there for you in the first phase of loss move on with life and it seems as if everyone around you has accepted that this is how it is now. This period, which is the phase we are now in, could be difficult. Whilst you would not want everyone to be reminding you of the traumatic event of that day, on the other hand you don't want them to forget that someone significant to you is missing. It's also difficult for those around you who could be in the wrong if they keep bringing up reminders of that day, yet it could be insensitive if they barely acknowledge it. It is not because they have forgotten but because they don't want to keep reminding you of it. It is more difficult for the immediate family.

I have heard of marriages breaking up after traumatic events such as this. Couples spend time blaming each other for the event or expecting the other partner to grieve in the same way as the other is grieving. We have to accept that we are all different when it comes to a lot of things, especially grief. One person grieves differently to another. It is normal for women to be more expressive in their grief but if you are the husband and your wife is not being expressive in her grieving, don't hold it against her, be supportive in whatever form she copes with her grief. There are even cultural differences in the way we grieve. In my African culture there is a more visible expression of grief compared to the British culture. It's important that we understand this and support each other in the way we express our grief. I could not imagine being separated from Trevor at this time. We have shared so many memories with Marley. Whilst he may express himself in a different way to me and I have felt this strong call to do the things I have been doing to help others, it does not mean that he loved Marley less or he does not want his memory to live on. I have to understand that it is my calling not his. Who knows if God may call him to do something later on? My advice to couples who may be going through something similar is to keep the communication going with each other and encourage each other.

I would like to encourage any parents who have gone through similar traumatic events of losing a child to avoid blaming each other or looking back and thinking if one or the other had been more accommodating this situation would not have happened. If you love each other don't make it worse by putting guilt on each other as it makes it harder to deal with the difficult emotions and loss that you would be feeling. You may have experienced other types of grief, like losing your parents or sibling but losing your child, for me, is so much worse in my opinion and I know because I have lost both parents and some of my siblings.

It does get bearable, though. I don't say better because I am not there yet. The physical pain which used to engulf me every time I think about Marley is not as sharp as it was. I remember attending a bereavement seminar in 2021 and one of the leaders shared this visual with us. When you lose someone the pain of the loss was symbolised with a beach ball and a glass bowl symbolised the capacity of the person who is bereaved. In the first few months, the image showed that the ball could not fit in the bowl because the person does not have the capacity to comprehend what happened. As time goes by the ball remains the same size but the capacity to comprehend what happened gets bigger. The image showed the size of the bowl gets bigger whilst the size of the ball remains the same, and over time it could fit completely in the bowl, not because the ball gets smaller but because the bowl gets bigger. There are books on loss and grief which could guide us; reading the testimonies of other people and experiencing the reality could be two completely different things. We have to trust God if we believe in Him, and if we don't, we must trust our instincts that we're doing the right things for all concerned, spouses, children and other affected parties. I do encourage all to trust in God because He has been such a tower of strength for me during these dark days. Proverbs 18: 10 The name of the LORD is a strong tower; The righteous runs to it and is safe and set on high [far above evil].

I want to iterate that mental health issues come in different forms; from what I have learnt in this short period of time since I lost Marley and continue to learn is that it is very important to seek early intervention if you are not sure. Get outside help, get professional expertise to make sense of what you or your loved one are experiencing. Parents do all you can to get younger children showing similar symptoms diagnosed to rule out any early stages of mental-health issues, since they are more receptive to intervention at an early age. There are lots of organizations out there who can support you.

Finally, I hope our story helps you cope with whatever difficult situation you are facing and draw strength and hope from our experience; indeed the dark clouds will get lighter and you will smile again.

Epilogue

Since the events covered in this book, a lot has happened. The foundation which I founded in May 2021 has now been registered as a charity in England and Wales. Prior to the registration Marley's Aart funded individual art therapy for a young boy between the ages of eight and ten. This was made possible because of the child trust fund which Marley never got to spend and the donations to the fundraising events, 7KG @7mths by Rosemary Peck and Marley's 8KM Memory Walk. Following the registration Marley's Aart has also funded group art therapy for six young people with mental health issues. We have also funded a workshop for parents and their children who are having anxiety and other mental health issues.

The foundation is making a difference funding art therapy for young people with mental health issues not only through CHUMS but more recently in schools. Starting with Marley's previous secondary school the foundation now funds individual and group art therapy for the students who have been suffering with anxiety and social disorder as well as transition and settling issues from primary to secondary school.

The second Marley's 8KM Memory Walk in December 2022 was well attended with 10% more people joining the local walk compared to the previous year. The number of locations where friends, family and supporters walked also increased compared to the previous year. When I started the foundation and planned the memory walk to coincide with Marley's birthdate, it was meant to be primarily a day for us to remember Marley publicly and to raise funds for his legacy. I did not foresee that the walk would raise awareness for others to check their mental health and be more open to talking to others about it. After the second walk I received feedback from people from different locations sharing how the walk created an opportunity for people to connect and talk about their feelings and who they could reach out to for help.

You can support the work Marley's Aart Foundation is funding by making donations on the website: www. marleysaartfoundation.com

Worldwide Organizations you could reach out to if you are concerned about the mental health of a loved one or you need to speak to someone:

CALM – Campaign Against Living Miserably
https://www.thecalmzone.net/international-mental-health-charities

CBM – Christian Blind Mission
https://www.cbmuk.org.uk/what-we-do/mental-health/

Choosing Therapy
https://www.choosingtherapy.com/top-mental-health-organizations/

MIND
https://www.mind.org.uk/

Acknowledgements

I am grateful to the support I have received from family, friends, my church Luton Christian Fellowship and the BSBS (Bedfordshire Suicide Bereavement Services) during these difficult months. Without the support of my husband Trevor and my son Nathan, I would not have written this second book. Above all I want to thank God for strengthening me and giving me a purpose, turning my pain to a purpose.

The Giraffes at Africa Live Zoo

Family At
Sea Life
Tunnel in
Great
Yarmouth
UK

The Lions
at the
Africa
Live Zoo